Build Your Confidence Through Wardrobe, Color & Style

By Diane B. Morris

Copyright © 2016 Diane B. Morris

All rights reserved.

ISBN-10: 1539569470
ISBN-13: 978-1539569473

This book is not intended as a substitute for the medical advice of physicians or clinicians. Readers should consult with a physician, dietitian, or other health care professional before beginning or making any changes to a diet, health, or exercise program. The authors and publisher expressly disclaim responsibility for any liability, loss, or risk—personal or otherwise—which is incurred, directly or indirectly, as a consequence of the use and application of any of the contents of this book.

All rights reserved. No part of this book may be reproduced, distributed or transmitted in any form or by any means, electronic or mechanical, including photocopying, recording, taping or by any information storage and retrieval system without permission in writing from the publisher, except in the case of reprints in the context of the reviews, quotes, or references for the inclusion of brief quotations in a review.

DEDICATION

This book is dedicated to:

My loving husband and best friend, Larry. Your patience and ongoing support fuels me to share my best self so that I can share my passions with the world.

My two children, Heather and Bryan and their spouses who are each committed to being their best selves in everything they do.

My three grandchildren who teach me to live adventurously. Their smiles reveal a ray of my sunshine every day.

TABLE OF CONTENTS

ACKNOWLEGMENTS

1	PERSONALITY	1
2	PERSONAL VISION	11
3	BEAUTY FOODS	17
4	OPTIMAL HEALTH	27
5	SUGAR CRAVINGS	41
6	STAND OUT	53
7	WARDROBE	57
8	COLOR	65
9	COLOR ANALYSIS	67
10	HAIR · SKIN · MAKEUP	73
11	STYLE	83
12	PERSONAL BRANDING	89

ABOUT THE AUTHOR

ACKNOWLEDGMENTS

There are many people who have touched my life in many ways, and I want to thank all of you.

You have inspired and motivated me throughout my journey to take a giant leap of faith to become an author. This book came to me through the inspiration and guidance from Linda Vettrus-Nichols. Her patience and professional skills made this book possible.

I would like to express a special thank you to my mother and father who worked long hours giving their utmost dedication to our family, synagogue and community. My parents' wishes were to assure our family was well taken care of in all areas of our lives. I wish to thank a special lady who came to live with our family shortly after World War II. She taught me resilience, love and spirit.

I would also like to thank my departed father in-law who trusted and supported me in everything I did. My mother-in-law who is a beacon of fashion and support. Our immediate family is eternally grateful for all of the wisdom they have both bestowed upon us.

Thank you to my siblings, extended family and many others including Rabbi Yossi Lew and family, Linda Segal, the late Susan Shapiro, Rachel Smartt, Abby Hirsch Phillips, Georgiann Voissem Micallef, Summer Turner and Pamela Bruner.

It is with equal gratitude that I acknowledge the women who have taken my course, shared with me their quest, and reawakened their authentic best self.

CHAPTER 1—PERSONALITY

YOU ARE YOUR BRAND

"We are all CEO's of our own companies...To be in business today, our most important job is to be head marketer for the brand called YOU".

-Tom Peters

How a person feels, acts and what they do in their daily life determines their personality. It is the total picture of what they stand for, how they view the world and how others perceive them.

Your Personality Brand

What is Personal Branding?

Personal Branding allows individuals to differentiate themselves by consistently communicating and leveraging their uniqueness.

If you are not branding yourself, you can be assured others are not doing it for you.

The Key to a Successful Personal Brand is a commitment to excellence, joy and happiness in your life. It's about partnering with individuals in a creative system that inspires you to maximize your potential, which is especially important in today's economy.

Personal branding is based on your personality, your life philosophy, dreams, values, identity, self-knowledge, self-awareness, self-responsibility, positive attributes and self-management. In other words, your authentic self, your authentic personal brand differs greatly from an invented false self and a false personal brand.

Selling a false brand to others does not work....

With an authentic personal brand, your strongest characteristics, attributes and values will separate you from the crowd. Without this, you look, speak and feel like everyone else in your industry and you certainly don't stand out when you enter a room.

This book is based on how I work with my clients to discover their personal brand from the inside out.

As an Image Consultant, the first place I start with my clients is to teach Personality Empowerment through Self-Awareness, Self-Discovery and Self-Compassion.

Self-Awareness

Authenticity leads to self-awareness, the ability to recognize one's existence including one's own traits, full potential and identity.

Self-awareness helps you to make wiser decisions. How and where you focus your attention and emotions determines where you are going in the future and how you go about living your daily life. Our emotions come from our perceptions as well as our personality traits. They affect our reactions as well as our behaviors and habits.

Our emotions appear without our assistance or help. If we don't allow ourselves to be aware of them—so that we can process, express and release them in a healthy way— our emotions can remain stuck inside and can do damage mentally and physically to our bodies.

Trapped emotions can become toxic to our mind and body. We often blame others for our emotions or things that go wrong because it is an easy and fast excuse. The problem here is that those types of reactions do not move us or the other person involved forward to a cooperative communication funnel.

Consciously changing the interpretation within our mind, of what is really going on, allows us to change our perception which then allows us to shift our emotions, whether they are positive or negative.

Maya Angelou once said, "When you know better, do better." Once you have made a mistake, learn from it and do better next time. Changing our thought patterns does not happen overnight because we are in a constant state of change adapting to our environment, cultural influences and our own individual experiences.

Learning how to shift our emotions is similar to how a muscle grows and strengthens. With time and effort the muscle gains strength and stamina.

Perceptions—Shifting our perceptions gives us the self-confidence to present our personal brand in a unique way and thus allows us to stand out in the crowd.

Self-awareness is developed through practice. Focusing our attention on the details of our unique personality, we can avoid behaviors such as putting ourselves down with negative self-talk. Believe me, it is not easy when your negative self-talk takes hold of you.

Yet your first step is to be aware of both positive and negative self-talk.

By recognizing your own positive and negative self-talk you can begin to understand other people and empathize with their emotions, thoughts and behaviors. When we feel grounded and good about ourselves, we are able to foster deeper and healthier personal and professional relationships.

When self-awareness leads to self-knowledge, positive change begins!!

The more we learn to be conscious of our impulses, thoughts and actions—while also keeping in mind our unique value principles—we slowly transform towards our best self every moment of the day.

Activity

Every time you think a negative thought or say a negative statement, reverse it and write down a positive statement starting with I AM…

For example with the statement or thought: "I can't do this." You would write or say: "I am able to accomplish _____ because I have the correct skills."

Self-Discovery

The key to a rewarding and productive life is to develop a specific plan that fulfills your personal vision. Discovering and implementing a personal vision is a process. It consists of learning about yourself, growing your relationships and continually fine-tuning your vision to help others be their best self by delivering your best self. It is a boomerang effect.

Your personal brand propels you forward and inspires those around you to reach their own dreams. I've learned this lesson in my own life.

If you don't identify your own brand, others will plan and direct your life for you.

As a Registered Licensed Dietitian, I've worked with many individuals who have not been faithful to who they are and in return used their weight as a 'cover up' to their repressed emotions and behaviors.

I am also an Image Consultant. It breaks my heart when people are not living as confidently as they could be. I know what it's like to not fit in, which really impacted my level of confidence and that's why I chose to specialize in Personal Branding.

I have included many tools in this book so you too can ignite your 'best' self—making a confident and lasting first impression.

Identifying Your Personal Brand

- Assess your personality
- Select your core values
- Write your vision statement
- Understand optimal health
- Learn how to stand out in a crowd
- Do a closet audit
- Evaluate your body & facial shape
- Learn how to flatter your body & face
- Do your color analysis
- Look at your skin care products and regimes
- Learn personal makeup tips
- Accessorize your wardrobe
- Evaluate your personal style

Activity

Now we are going to do a visualization of your 'best self'.

Sit comfortably and close your eyes. You are now visualizing where you are in your personal life and business one year from today….the visualization will last **for 2 minutes**. Set a timer, close your eyes, take 2 deep breaths and relax.

What does your future life and/or business look and feel like to you? How are you acting in response to this life?

What are you feeling?

What does it smell like?

What time of day is it?

Who are you with?

What are you wearing?

Where are you?

The more you stay out of logic, the stronger the visualization is because you are now starting to build your new 'best' brain cells.

Use this energy, step into the feeling, smells, lighting, the time of day, your appearance, etc.

Keep your eyes closed. Breathe and relax….

What came up for you?

Do this activity at least once a day to really embed your future best self in your brain.

Self-Compassion

Compassion is about being kind and understanding with others. Self-compassion is about being kind and understanding with ourselves.

We all have weaknesses and we all have strengths. As women we tend to add compassion and kindness to the world around us but when it comes to ourselves we just can't seem to feel it or we can't recognize it or we can't respect ourselves or feel like we've earned it.

When we open the door for somebody or let them pass by in the grocery store line or tell someone how grateful we are that they are in our life—all of those actions are acts of kindness.

Why is it that we are compassionate when we want to help fellow-strugglers, but we often struggle to feel the same compassion toward ourselves when we face our own struggles?

Why do we often criticize ourselves, sometimes harshly, when we mess up and fall? Why are we so much tougher on ourselves when it comes to our faults and flaws? It is the old conversation in our head telling us that we are not good enough, nor worthy of our own self-compassion.

Yet somewhere buried underneath is a person who knows that it is possible for you to be happy, content and successful.

There are countless possible reasons why we find fault with ourselves when we fall short of our compassionate emotions. Most of us have heard and accepted these words in our mind, "Don't show your weaknesses."

Self-compassion is a willingness to look at our shortcomings with kindness and understanding. Making mistakes is human. Being gentle, supportive and understanding of oneself is what moves us forward.

Self-compassion is about taking care of your own needs. It's about nurturing yourself—physically, emotionally, mentally and spiritually. It's about saying that you are a valid person on this planet.

Once we develop true self-compassion, we quit comparing ourselves to others and become more focused on striving to make our life better.

Rather than critically judging ourselves for personal weaknesses, we can offer warmth and unconditional acceptance towards ourselves. We get to realize that it is perfectly fine and actually a universal law, to be imperfect.

When we criticize ourselves, such as "I feel so stupid." our negative self-talk lowers our self-confidence which causes us to feel anxious, stressed, angry and sad.

Brain cell connections start during our childhood years so it is not always easy to recognize negative emotions that prompt negative self-talk.

Steps Toward Self-Compassion

1. Acknowledge your weaknesses.

2. Find ways to soothe and comfort yourself in times of adversity ie. Listening to music, meditation, massage, deep breathing, etc.

3. Ask yourself what would be the wisest, most constructive self-talk at any given moment?

4. Give yourself permission to treat yourself kindly.

I used to think that I needed to be a 'people pleaser' so people would recognize and accept me.

People pleasing, in my mind, would also keep my

imperfections from being noticed. Some people cover their faults with alcohol, drugs, bullying at school or by displaying prejudice behaviors. I tended to retreat into my own world and get lost in my books.

Mindfulness

Mindfulness is part of practicing self-compassion. Seeing things as they are, being aware of your own negativity and the willingness to change is to have compassion for yourself as well as others. Yet if you don't notice your negative self-talk, you won't feel the negativity and are unable to heal. Mindfulness also allows us to think about what is true and gives us the space to question whether it is true or not. It gives us a chance to respond reflectively instead of reactively.

An example of a typical scenario in regards to mindfulness: You've left numerous messages for a prospect, you may start to think they are not interested in you or that you may have said something that offended them. You have a choice here. You can assume the worst or you can fill your heart with positive energy and give them the benefit of your doubts. They may have been busy or had something else in their life that is taking a higher priority. We tend to go to a negative thought pattern when we are feeling rejected or inadequate.

CHAPTER 2—PERSONAL VISION

There are many definitions of values that are found in the dictionary. What resonates with me is: Values are a belief, a mission or a philosophy that is meaningful to you. Whether we are consciously aware of them or not, each individual has a core set of personal values and those core values are the foundation for creating a personal vision statement.

Values develop from many pathways. They start within our family units, move on into our religious or spiritual beliefs, school experiences and now more than ever our social media preferences. **Values generate behaviors to assist in answering questions of why people do what they do and what order they choose to do them in.**

According to Marketing Professor and Sociologist Morris Massey, values are developed during 3 significant periods in a person's life: Birth to 7 years, 8 to 13 years, and 14 to 21 years of age.

Our values are developed from our beliefs and convictions which then guide and direct our thoughts, actions and behaviors.

Core Values

Core values are part of our personality. When our life priorities are aligned with our core values we are on our way to experience a positive fulfillment in our life. Our core values are a central part of who we are.

I give my clients a core values identification sheet which is a list of 135 words, for example:

Acceptance	Discovery	Elegance	Happiness	Loyalty
Peacefulness	Reliability	Serenity	Trust	Fun

They select 25 core values that resonate with them and place those words into 5 categories: Emotional, Physical, Spiritual, Financial and Social. These are the 5 areas that all humans seek when looking to find balance.

Then I have them create their personal vision statement.

Personal Vision Statement

This statement is written in first person and constructed as if this statement is already happening in one's life. I have my clients choose as many of their core value words from the 5 categories to effectively write their statement.

I let my clients know that it won't be a final product because they will keep refining their personal vision statement as they step into their future life experiences.

Having a clear personal vision statement provides the direction necessary to design the choices a person makes about their life. A personal vison statement illuminates the way towards personal confidence and success. Life becomes more satisfying when we are positively connected in our relationships and life experiences.

I've included my personal vision statement here:

"I am physically and nutritionally fit by consuming a whole plant based diet and exercising at least 4 times/week, actively involved in a heart based marriage and career that involves gratitude, love, compassion and acceptance of who I am. My leadership skills include trust, reliability, encouragement and consideration for others to influence them to pursue their dreams. My confidence grows every moment with my courage, personal development, expertise and self-discovery. My core values offer me serenity, harmony, security, peace of mind and greater wealth to serve others with the work that I love."

A personal vision statement serves as a major focus for prioritizing daily, monthly and yearly activities. The final and most important reason for writing a personal vision statement is that it moves you forward more effectively towards your goals, passions and dreams. It is the essence of who you are.

I have a special gift for you…

A complimentary copy of my

Core Values Identification Sheet

Email me at: diane@dianebmorris.com to receive your copy. Just tell me where to send it.

CHAPTER 3—BEAUTY FOODS & BEVERAGES

Your diet affects your day-to-day appearance. Your body reveals what you put in your mouth, whether it is healthy food or not. Creating a healthy lifestyle allows for better mobility and gives you a healthier glow. It's the recipe to looking gorgeous and feeling fantastic for years to come.

The term 'beauty foods' has hit the media recently. You may have heard about 'superfoods' and their function to fight free radicals and toxins from our foods and environment. Beauty foods follow the same health suit as superfoods. Beauty foods provide essential nutrients specifically designed to fight against wrinkles and give your skin a special healthy glow.

Beauty foods are full of nutrient-dense vitamins, minerals and antioxidants (phytonutrients). They have been proven to boost overall health and aid in weight loss. The individual parts of our bodies are all interconnected. Millions of cells are relying on you to nourish them well so they can function at their highest level to improve and maintain your optimal health.

Collagen and elastin are proteins which give elasticity and firmness to our cells. Collagen is a vital fibrous protein found in the connective tissue of the body. It connects and supports skin tissue, bones, muscles, tendons, cartilage, organs, blood vessels and our gastrointestinal tract. Collagen works with other proteins such as keratin and elastin to add flexibility. When an individual loses collagen in their body, they develop wrinkles.

Elastin gives elasticity to our tissues. In addition to being found in the skin, elastin is found in organs and other parts of the body, including the spaces between tissues. It forms an integrated bundle (like a strong spider web of proteins) to support the organs and structural components which include blood vessels, the heart and lungs. Elastin allows individuals to participate in high-intensity activities such as running—without damage to internal organs.

Beauty Foods & Beverages that promote healthy glowing skin and cellular integrity…

Beverages

Organic Rose Water

Helps improve skin conditions such as acne and rosacea. Apply to skin to soothe the red spots because it has an anti-inflammatory effect.

Green Tea

Selecting green tea can be confusing because there are several different forms including Matcha powder, tea bags and tea leaves. Your healthiest option is to use Matcha, which is a more concentrated, powdered form of green tea. One cup of green tea made with Matcha powder has the same nutritional value as drinking 10 cups of regular brewed tea. Add 1 teaspoon of the Matcha powder to a tea cup. Pour hot water that is just under a boil into the cup.

Never use boiling water when making green tea. If the water temperature gets to a boil, green tea becomes too bitter and its delicate aroma and flavor is lost. Stir and enjoy! If you would like to sweeten it, add 5 drops of Stevia or a bit of raw honey. Drink the tea immediately, as it will get bitter if it sits for a while. In a study published in the Journal of Nutrition in 2011, people who drank a beverage containing green tea daily for 12 weeks had skin that was more elastic and smooth and had one quarter less sun damage when exposed to UV light as compared to a control group. The tea's antioxidants boost blood flow and oxygen to the skin, which delivers key nutrients to keep the skin protected.

Fruits

Orange Peel

Researchers from the University of Arizona looked at

people who reported that they consumed citrus fruits, juices and peels weekly. People who ate orange peel or lemon zest had a 33% decreased risk of squamous cell carcinoma, a type of skin cancer. The juice did not have any effect. Limonene, an antioxidant found in the oil in the peels offered UV protection benefits. The peels can be dried and used as a mild face and body rub for clean and softer skin. Orange, lemon, lime and grapefruit peels can all be saved for future use. First, remove the colored part of the peel with a zester or a sharp knife. Then choose a method to dry the peels. Lay the peels on a rack and air-dry them on your kitchen counter or spread the peels out on a tray. You can dry peels in a traditional oven on low heat (150 degrees) for several hours or even overnight. Food dehydrators designed to dry fruits and vegetables are very easy to use. Once peels are dry, place in a clean container with a tight-fitting lid and store in a cool, dry spot. To use, grind the dried peels in a food processor or coffee grinder until they resemble coarse flour.

Citrus Fruits

Citrus fruits help to fight inflammation and are a rich natural source of vitamin C—essential for healthy bodies, skin and hair. Citrus fruits also contain B vitamins and inositol—both necessary for healthy skin and hair. To help reduce age spots, use fresh lemon juice to safely fade and remove dark patches from your skin. Rub lemon juice on the spot with a cotton ball twice daily, and in six to eight weeks you should see a difference.

Grapes

Contain Resveratrol which is in the skin of grapes and helps to fight inflammation. Research shows it may fight the effects of UV light and sun damage. This antioxidant helps to improve memory.

Coconut and Coconut Water

This fruit contains copper, which helps to promote glowing skin. The meat of the coconut helps balance our hormones, improves skin texture, hair texture and body metabolism. Scrape the coconut meat out of the coconut and freeze it for a delicious icy dessert. Researchers at the University of Geneva found that when 1 to 2 tablespoons of coconut oil were consumed each day, energy expenditure increased and helped subjects to burn approximately 120 calories a day.

Not all coconut oil is created equal, so you'll want to be selective about the type you purchase. When you are shopping, you will see two main categories of coconut oil: refined and unrefined. The refined coconut oil will not have the coconut taste, because it has been altered from its original form. You can start using coconut oil where you might usually use canola oil or butter. For example, if you are using a recipe that calls for 3 tablespoons of canola oil, try using 3 tablespoons of refined coconut oil instead.

Kiwi

Kiwi contains nearly 120% of your daily needs of Vitamin C—in one medium kiwi. Vitamin C stimulates collagen synthesis. A study in the American Journal of Clinical Nutrition found that a diet high in Vitamin C was related to less dryness and less noticeable wrinkles.

Chocolate

Dark Chocolate

The flavanols in dark chocolate act as antioxidants, provide sun protection and reduce the roughness of skin for a healthier appearance and feel. Avoid chocolates with chocolate liquor as one of the ingredients.

Cacao

Contains one of the highest level of antioxidants and vitamin C. Add raw organic cacao powder to a smoothie. Cacao chips are great when added to a healthy crunch trail mix.

Nuts and Seeds

Almonds

Almonds contain vitamin E, an antioxidant that defends against sun damage. Those who eat several servings of nuts per week are less likely to gain extra pounds.

Chia Seeds

Chia seeds are rich in omega 3 essential fatty acids that help erase blemishes and soften wrinkles. These seeds also help to keep the skin hydrated and supple. They are a great source of overall hydration and assist in regularity. Chia seeds can easily be soaked in water for 5 minutes or placed in smoothies.

Sunflower Seeds

These seeds are rich in selenium which preserves elastin to keep skin smooth and tight. Selenium acts as an antioxidant. Sunflower seeds also contain vitamin E which works well with selenium to enhance the effects of both.

Walnuts

Deficiencies in omega 3 fatty acids (alpha linolenic acid) can result in dry scaly skin or even eczema. Walnuts are the only type of nut that contain a significant amount of omega 3 fatty acids.

Vegetables

Romaine Lettuce

Romaine lettuce is very high in vitamin A and moderate in

Vitamin C. Both vitamins help to improve skin and hair. A 2 cup serving of romaine lettuce provides 164% of your daily vitamin A requirement and 38% of your daily vitamin C needs! It's one of the best loved lettuces for providing a mild, non-bitter taste.

Sweet Potatoes

These orange tubers are packed with carotenoids and vitamin C which boost collagen production. Collagen controls the strength, firmness and flexibility of the skin.

Peppers

Red bell peppers contain antioxidants and more vitamin C than found in oranges. The spicier peppers come packed with capsaicin, a compound that improves circulation and promotes the release of toxins from the skin. Red peppers have more vitamin C than green or even orange peppers.

Tomatoes

(technically a fruit because they have seeds)

Lycopene, the compound that gives tomatoes their rich red color, is a powerful antioxidant that eliminates skin-aging free radicals from ultraviolet exposure. Fruits and vegetables rich in carotenoids also color our skin and give it a healthful glow.

Pumpkins

(technically a fruit because they have seeds)

Cooked pumpkin is one of the top sources of beta-carotene. The body converts beta-carotene into vitamin A—a half-of-a-cup of cooked pumpkin supplies more than 350% of your daily needs for Vitamin A, keeping skin soft and smooth with less wrinkles.

Kale

Kale is one of the best sources of lutein and zeaxanthin. These antioxidants absorb and neutralize free radicals created by UV light including the wavelengths that sneak through sunscreen and reach your skin. One cup of kale gives you 134% of vitamin C and 133% of your daily value for A, both necessary for skin firming. One of the easiest ways to get greens into your diet daily is to add them to a fruit smoothie.

Raw Green Smoothies

This may sound unappealing, but when you add raw greens into a smoothie, such as spinach or swiss chard, you can't taste them. If you find that collard greens or kale taste bitter, like I do, you can blanch them in boiling water for a couple of minutes before sautéing them. To do this, bring a pot of water to a boil, add your greens to the pot, let them cook for two minutes, drain in a colander and then sauté in a pan with coconut oil. The best way to choose your leafy greens is by looking at the color—the darker the better. Darker vegetables have higher levels of antioxidants and nutrients so they keep you feeling full for a longer period of time. If you want to supercharge your nutrition, start adding collard greens, cabbage, kale and bok choy to your diet. These dark, leafy greens are also cruciferous vegetables so they pack a powerful nutritional boost. They are heartier and contain more fiber than other greens.

Cultured Vegetables

Kimchi, sauerkraut and fermented vegetables work very well because they are probiotics. Probiotics help to clean the gut, liver and blood. They also detox and support your skin.

Meats

Grass Fed Beef

Grass fed beef contains a higher ratio of omega 3 to omega 6 fatty acids which reduces inflammation and contains the building blocks of collagen and elastin. Lean choices include sirloin and flank steak.

CHAPTER 4—OPTIMAL HEALTH

Practicing self-care and identifying your optimal health needs are both vital to uncovering your authentic best self and igniting your personal brand. Self-care is more than Me Time. It involves adequate hydration, carbohydrates, protein, fat, fiber, fruits and vegetables.

Hydration

We all know the importance of drinking water.

You may not be aware there are at least 12 reasons why we should stay hydrated:

1. Regulates body temperature

2. Blood contains 83% water

3. Bones contain 22% water

4. Brain contains 50% water

5. Muscles contain 75% water

6. Transports nutrients and oxygen to the cells

7. Moisturizes the air in our lungs

8. Helps with body metabolism

9. Helps organs to absorb nutrients more efficiently

10. Protects organs

11. Protects and moisturizes joints

12. Detoxifies

How much water does your body need daily?

Simple calculation: Take your weight and divide by 2. This sum/number is the amount of water that your body needs. For example, for someone weighing 100 pounds, dividing 100 by 2 would = 50 ounces of water. There are 8 ounces in a cup so 50 divided by 8 = 6 cups and 3 ounces. This person needs 6 cups and 3 ounces of water daily in order to stay hydrated.

FYI: Water is not soda pop, juice, tea or coffee.

Easy ways to get your daily water needs:

- Keep 1 cup (8 ounces) of water with lemon juice by your bed side and drink upon waking

- Drink water every 15 minutes while exercising to replace water depletion

- Drink water in between meals but only sip water throughout meals

- AVOID diet beverages and beverages with high calories

- Flavor your water with herbal tea or fruit pieces
- Drink water through a straw
- Always carry a water bottle with you for easy access
- Set a water alarm to remind yourself to drink

Timing for drinking water (1 glass = 8 ounces)

- 2 glasses of water 30 minutes before breakfast, lunch and dinner helps with digestion
- 1 glass of water before and after taking a bath or shower helps keep you hydrated
- 1 glass of water before going to bed helps to prevent stroke or heart attack

The top water rich foods include:

Cucumbers	96% water
Lettuce	96% water
Watercress	90% water
Watermelon	96% water
Celery	95% water
Tomatoes	94% water
Broccoli	92% water
Spinach	92% water

Carrots	90% water
Grapefruit	90% water

Nutrition

Vitamins & Minerals

Vitamins and minerals are essential for our development and wellbeing. Vitamins and minerals are not naturally produced in the human body.

Nutritional deficiencies can have devastating effects on our body and health. The grave nature of this problem can be estimated through the fact that almost half of the world's children, between 6 months to five years of age, suffer from one or more deficiencies pertaining to vitamins and minerals.

In total, more than 2 billion individuals are affected from this deficiency on an annual basis.

Vitamins are classified as either fat soluble (Vitamins A, D, E and K) or water soluble Vitamins (C, B12, thiamin, niacin, riboflavin, tryptophan, pantothenic acid, biotin and folic acid).

This difference between the two groups is very important. It determines how each vitamin acts within the body.

The fat soluble vitamins are soluble in lipids (fats). These vitamins are usually absorbed in fat globules (called chylomicrons) that travel through the lymphatic system of the small intestines and into the general blood circulation within the body. These fat soluble vitamins, especially vitamins A and E, are then stored in body tissues.

If a person takes in too much of a fat soluble vitamin, over time they can have too much of that vitamin present in their body.

People can also be deficient in a fat soluble vitamin if their fat intake is too low or if their fat absorption is compromised, for example, by certain drugs that interfere with the absorption of fat from the intestine or by certain diseases.

Unlike fat soluble vitamins, water soluble vitamins dissolve in water. They are quickly absorbed into the blood stream and transported to body tissues. These vitamins are not stored and are easily excreted from the body, so we require them on a daily basis.

No single fruit or vegetable provides all of the nutrients you need to be healthy.

Benefits of Eating Plenty of Fruits and Vegetables

A diet rich in vegetables and fruits can lower blood pressure, reduce risk of heart disease and stroke, prevent some types of cancer, lower risk of eye and digestive problems and have a positive effect upon blood sugar which can help keep one's appetite in check.

Eat a variety of types and colors of produce in order to give your body the mix of nutrients it needs. Try dark leafy greens, brightly colored red, yellow and orange vegetables and fruits.

Vegetables hydrate your skin, which can help reduce wrinkles. Not only are some vegetables 85 to 95 percent water, they also contain a plethora of phytonutrients that help guard against aging by preventing cell damage from stress, ultraviolet light and environmental toxins.

Vegetables also provide you with omega 3 fats and B vitamins, proven to help reduce anxiety and depression.

Fruits and vegetables make up a huge part of a healthy diet. They contain essential vitamins, minerals and antioxidants that keep your body functioning well and protect it against harmful free radicals.

Carbohydrates

Carbohydrates are our body's primary and preferred source of energy. Our brain and red blood cells rely exclusively on carbohydrates for fuel. They provide energy to the body, especially the brain.

Not all carbohydrates are created equal.

Two Categories of Carbohydrates/Carbs

Carbs are broken down to a simple form of energy called glucose, which either gets used right away for fuel or is stored and ready for use within 24 - 48 hours. Any extra sugar (glucose) is transformed into fat for later use.

The more carbs you eat, the higher the glucose levels are in the blood stream.

The two categories of carbs are **Complex** and **Simple**.

The Complex Carbs release sugar slowly and are often referred to as Slow Carbs. They burn slowly because they have a higher level of nutrition—can include vitamins, minerals, protein, fiber and fats. These are the carbs that help to maintain healthy blood sugar levels.

Complex/Slow Carbs: Whole grains, vegetables, legumes (starches), beans, glycogen, dextrose (sugar used in food), wheat, flours/breads, whole wheat cereals, cracked wheat, oatmeal, whole cornmeal, barley, brown rice, wild rice, buckwheat, popcorn, rye, quinoa, amaranth, millet and sorghum.

Benefits of Complex Carbohydrates

- Decrease anxiety, depression and anger
- Keep your memory sharp
- Can prevent weight gain

The Simple Carbs release sugar quickly and are often referred to as Fast Carbs. They burn quickly because they have little to no nutritional value. These carbs raise blood sugar levels within 2 hours or less. When the blood sugar drops the body signals the brain that it's time to eat again. Combine simple carbs with nutritious foods, protein, good fats or fiber to slow them down.

Simple or Refined/Fast Carbs: Fruit, sugar, honey, naturally occurring sugars and manmade added sugars in cakes and pies, candies, white flour pastas, tortillas, fructose (fruit sugar), lactose (milk sugar), mannose, maltose (beer, vegetables), sucrose (table sugar), and glucose (brown sugar, agave, high fructose corn syrup).

The Blood Sugar Story

All carbs, whether they are complex or simple, digest the same. Cellular changes occur which convert their sugars into a usable form of energy called glucose.

INSULIN, a hormone, is released by the pancreas and is responsible for transporting glucose out of the blood stream into our cells for short or long term storage. Specifically, insulin delivers glucose to our working muscles and brain to be used as fuel for immediate responses.

To maintain a healthy weight without having your mood turn into 'Godzilla', a decreased energy level and/or brain fog—is to consume the complex/slow carbohydrates and pair your carbs with lean protein and good fats.

Protein

Protein makes up about 20% of your body weight and is a primary component of our muscles, hair, nails, skin, eyes and internal organs—especially the heart and brain.

Our immune system requires protein for the formation of antibodies that help fight infections, manufacture hormones and enzymes and preserve the proper acid-alkali pH balance in the body.

Lean proteins should be consumed with every meal!

Benefits of Protein

- Helps maintain muscle while you lose fat
- Prevents you from feeling hungry
- Helps control appetite and blood sugar

Healthy Choices for Protein

Ground Beef (90% or Leaner)
Lean ground beef is a source of high-quality protein. 3 ounces delivers plenty of iron, zinc and vitamin B12 so you don't need a lot of lean ground beef in your meal to get enough protein.

Vegetarian Proteins Are Super-Healthy
Eat vegetarian proteins frequently. Not only are they a healthy protein they provide fiber, heart-healthy folate and energy-creating iron.

Low fat or Nonfat Dairy
Milk, yogurt, cottage cheese and ricotta cheese are good lean sources of protein. Make a smoothie with yogurt, skim milk and your favorite fruits for a healthy on-the-go breakfast or snack. Top whole grain toast with skim ricotta, a drizzle of honey, pumpkin seeds and lemon zest for a delicious, wholesome breakfast.

Fish & Shellfish
Most Americans don't eat enough fish. The American Heart Association recommends aiming for at least two 3.5-oz servings per week. Keep cans of light tuna and wild Alaskan salmon on hand. They both make a great sandwich filling and salad toppers. Salmon cakes are a delicious way to eat salmon, especially if you find salmon too rich tasting.

Tofu & Other Soy Foods
Great vegetarian protein sources. A ½ cup of tofu gives you 8 - 10 grams of protein (depending on whether it's soft or firm). 1 cup of edamame gives you 17 grams of protein. Edamame also packs a whopping 8 grams of fiber. Calcium-set tofu gives you a healthy dose of bone-building calcium.

Nuts, Nut Butters & Seeds
Unless you're allergic to them, nuts and seeds are a must-have in your diet. A Harvard research study found that nuts and seeds are one of the top foods linked to weight loss. Plus they are chocked full of healthy fats, fiber and protein. Natural peanut or almond butters are a great choice for topping your morning toast. Toss pumpkin and sunflower seeds together with dried fruit for an energizing afternoon snack.

Pork Loin
Pork tenderloin, loin chops and sirloin roast are lean cuts of pork. A 3-oz. serving of pork chops, for instance, gives you 23 grams of protein and a bounty of energy-

producing B vitamins (thiamin, niacin, B6 and B12), along with 2 grams of saturated fat.

Eggs

The incredible, edible egg is a good way to get nutritious protein in your diet. Just one egg offers 6 grams of protein and only 70 calories. Note: Most of that protein is in the egg white.

Elimination

The best way to get waste out of the body efficiently is to hydrate well and eat enough fiber.

Fiber

Choosing high fiber foods has become confusing and brings up many questions.

- What's the difference between all of the fiber types?
- Which type should I choose with my meals?
- Are processed grains high in fiber?

Benefits of Fiber

- Promotes gut health
- Prevents constipation & hemorrhoids

- Helps reduce developing many chronic diseases

- Lowers the risk of cancers, especially colon and breast cancer

- Helps to lower LDL cholesterol (bad cholesterol) and total cholesterol

Furthermore, high-fiber foods help in managing Type 2 diabetes because they slow digestion and keep blood sugar stable.

Tip: Slowly increase fiber in your diet by adding 5 grams daily. Adding too much fiber too quickly can be linked to constipation. It's important to give your digestive system time to get used to the additional roughage.

A gram is the size and weight of a paper clip.

Guidelines for fiber…

- 38 grams daily for men under age 50

- 30 grams daily for men over age 50

- 25 grams daily for women under age 50

- 21 grams daily for women over age 50

2 Types of Fiber: Soluble Fiber and Insoluble Fiber

Both soluble and insoluble fiber go undigested and are not absorbed into the bloodstream. Fiber content is often listed under 'Total Carbohydrates' on a food product label called a Nutrition Facts Label. Because fiber goes undigested, it contains 0 calories.

Our bodies use fiber for elimination rather than energy.

Soluble fiber forms a sticky gel when mixed with liquid, and helps to remove cholesterol plaque while lowering total cholesterol and LDL cholesterol (bad cholesterol) therefore reducing the risk of heart disease. Soluble fiber regulates blood sugar. It also decreases appetite because of the slow emptying of the stomach.

Insoluble fiber passes through the intestines, mostly intact, thus preventing constipation. It also removes toxic waste from the colon and keeps our bowel movements regular. Insoluble fiber helps prevent colon cancer by keeping an optimal pH in our intestines which prevents microbes from producing cancerous substances.

Generally, when it comes to fiber, the darker the color, the higher the fiber content. Fill your shopping cart with: carrots, beets, broccoli, collard greens, swiss chard, spinach, artichokes, potatoes (russet, red, and sweet).

Fats

Eat Protein and Healthy Fats at Each Meal

The low-fat diet craze caused people to fear all sources of dietary fat, including the healthy fats that our bodies need to function properly.

To make up for the lack of fat and taste in their products, food companies add more SUGAR! Low fat foods are not very satisfying, which causes even more hunger. This leads to grabbing other foods and more calories, which are not good if your end goal is weight loss.

Benefits of Eating Healthy Fats

- Provides essential fatty acids
- Carries vital nutrients, vitamins and minerals
- Creates a source of energizing fuel

Good Fat

Unsaturated fats—include polyunsaturated and monounsaturated. Good fat promotes heart and brain health. These include fish oil, flax oil, olive oil, tuna, salmon, herring, nut oils and tree nuts.

Unsaturated fats are critical components of brain cell membranes and are needed for the production and proper functioning of neurotransmitters—the chemical messengers that our brain cells use in order to communicate.

Avoid partially hydrogenated oils, which are chemically processed oils such as: corn oil, cottonseed oil, palm kernel oil, sunflower oil, safflower oil and soybean oil.

CHAPTER 5—SUGAR CRAVINGS

Get Out of Sugar Jail

I am an Image Consultant and Registered Licensed Dietitian. Throughout my 29 years of nutrition practice, medical research and real life experiences, I began to connect the dots and realized that a woman's weight, mood, brain fog, fatigue, gluten sensitivity and emotional symptoms are directly related to—uncontrollable real and artificial sugar cravings. I faced them every day myself, now I manage to crush them and keep them under control. That's why I wrote the book: *Get Out of Sugar Jail* in order to pass this information on to others.

My passion involves helping individuals take control of their body through proven nutrition practices, mindset and lifestyle adjustments to secure an overall permanent health balance.

My issues with sugar began early in my life.

My Past

A wonderful lady lived with our family for over 30 years. She helped take care of my siblings and me while our Mom and Dad worked in their neighborhood grocery store. Every Wednesday she walked to the bus to go downtown, completed her errands and came home with bags of candies to fill her 'magical' candy drawer in her bedroom dresser. The wonderful tasting large German Dark Chocolate bars, Brach's Candies and chewing gum were just a few of the things she carefully placed in this drawer. She often shared her treats with us. So at a very young age, my sweet tooth began to develop. When I was 10 years old, 8 cavities were discovered during one dentist visit! This was one result of my own sugar addiction.

For most of my young adult life, I could eat whatever I wanted and stay a 'normal' weight. My body had no trouble metabolizing sugar, or any other foods because my nutrition knowledge helped to keep the pounds off. However, when I hit my forties I gained weight and noticed my waistline expanding. My hips were rounder, and it was tough to keep my belly tucked in despite exercising 3 times a week—walking, sit ups, water aerobics, floor exercise programs, etc.

I experimented with low fat, high fat, low carb, no carb and high protein diet rages. I still noticed the nagging belly fat persisting.

At that time, I didn't realize how sugar and artificial

sweeteners caused belly fat, irritability, memory issues and the uncontrollable urges to crave even more sugar!

Tips I Discovered to Avoid Sugar Cravings

If you want to make good choices, only keep good choices in the house. Keep the veggies and fruit at eye level and in plain view for the children to see. When they see healthier choices first, they go for what's within easy reach. Keep washed, pre-cut veggies with a yummy dip ready to eat. Stock your pantry with whole foods with fiber to satisfy your hunger and give your body the best nutrition it needs. This greatly aids to the reduction of cravings, because you won't feel so hungry.

My Future

I am honored and excited to help individuals finally conquer their struggles with sugar cravings so they can achieve a level of vibrant energy, confidence and joy by getting out of their own personal sugar jail.

One of My Favorite Quotes

"I need insulin to stay alive. It's just therapy to keep going. What I can do is make sure that I keep my blood sugar down to a reasonable level. I can exercise and I can eat properly..."

-Mary Tyler Moore

Cravings

Cravings are something all of us struggle with at times so you're not alone if this is something you're dealing with too.

Cravings can be triggered by many things including: sights, sounds, aromas, your environment, stress and more. A perfect example of this is a typical trip to the local mall. We can easily be triggered when walking by the chocolate chip cookie business or cinnamon roll shop—this scenario involves sights, sounds and aromas from a previous environment/memory. Another example that is common for a lot of people is that cravings can come from stress of a deadline, stress when faced with something they dislike for example doing their taxes or balancing their check book. Another trigger is boredom.

Since our appetite and our eating habits do not exist in a bubble, experiences that are part of our daily lives can trigger cravings.

The more we understand our cravings, the better equipped we are to deal with them constructively.

It's not realistic to think you will NEVER eat sugar, but the reality is that most people are consuming WAY too much added sugar in their diets. Sugar is in SO many of the foods we eat and we usually aren't even aware of it (breads, crackers, sauces, chips). The worst part of it is that sugar can be quite addictive.

Your Cravings Are Not Always Your Fault

We are inundated every day with foods that are high in calories and low in nutrients. Fast food, packaged food, junk food and restaurant menus can be very deceiving. Fruit juice may have more sugar than a bottle of Coca Cola! We're ultimately paying the price with our health and our waistlines. When we consume processed foods/nutrient-void foods, our body knows it's not getting what it needs so it craves more and signals us to eat more and more and more. We actually begin to crave foods with empty calories that are deficient in necessary nutrients.

Sugar

The average American consumes about 150 lbs. of sugar per year. That's 12.5 lbs. a month or almost 3 lbs. a week. It's hard to imagine it's that much! However, you may be thinking you're not part of the average group because you really don't eat that many sweets. The real problem is that the majority of sugar we consume is hidden in processed and fast foods, cereals, snacks and white flour products—it's even in salad dressings, sauces and beverages! Gluten free foods tend to have sugar as well. Even products labeled 'healthy' are often loaded with sugar.

About 15% of the calories in the American adult diet come from added sugars. That's about 22 teaspoons of added sugar a day! Sugar is usually added to make foods and drinks taste better. Unfortunately such foods can be high in calories and offer none of the health benefits that fruits and other naturally sweet foods do.

Sugar makes us feel happy, energetic and it can even make us feel calm sometimes.

Here's Why

The sugar breakdown starts in the mouth and sends signals to the brainstem. From there it goes to another part of the brain that releases dopamine, a neurotransmitter. Dopamine is our 'feel good/reward' chemical. This pleasure center is the same center where alcohol, heroin and cocaine are stimulated. Just when you were feeling 'up', you are likely going to feel worse than you did before you had that sugar rush after your blood sugar crashes. So as a result, you want and need even more. It can be a hard cycle to break.

During this immediate sensation, dopamine (a chemical messenger) quickly signals another part of the brain to implant a 'memory bank' for future pleasure. Thus, our cravings and addictions continue in a vicious cycle.

Our brain needs constant fuel (like gas in our car). Gas = glucose. The brain does not have the capacity to store glucose. It is the amount of sugar we consume per day beyond the recommended amount that gets us into sugar jail, an addictive state of craving sugar.

The 2016 American Dietary guidelines recommend we consume less than 10 percent of our daily intake of calories from 'added sugars', as a target to help us meet our nutritional needs, without going over our calorie limit.

Added sugars are sugars added by food manufacturers.

There is a great article titled, *Food Cravings Engineered by Industry*, which details how big food companies keep us eating through a combination of science and marketing. Copy this link into your browser to learn more if you're interested:

 http://www.cbc.ca/news/health/food-cravings-engineered-by-industry-1.1395225

Of course there are many possible causes for cravings including but not limited to stress, nutrient deficiencies, hormone imbalances and fluctuations in blood sugar levels.

When it comes to sugar in foods and beverages, your brain's response is to send the signal to eat more. You might think this is the perfect reason to consume artificially sweetened foods, however this isn't true. When you eat a sweet food item that doesn't carry any calories, your brain gets confused. It thinks you are starving. This causes you to crave even more sweets.

The American Heart Association recommends a maximum of 26 grams of sugar for women and 37 grams of sugar for men per day.

Added Sugar in Soda (per 12 ounces of soda)

- Lemon-lime soda contains 37.6 grams
- Ginger ale contains 31.8 grams
- Cola has 38.9 grams
- Pepper-type soda varieties contain 38.2 grams
- Root beer contains 39.2 grams
- **Cream soda is among the worst choices** with 49.3 grams per serving
- Grape and orange-flavored sodas
- Keep in mind that if you drink a 16-ounce or 20-ounce bottle of soda, your intake of sugar will be much higher.

    Adapted from Sara Ipatenco, Demand Media
    healthyeating.sfgate.com

Artificial Sugar Studies:

One study performed MRI's on volunteers while they took sips of water sweetened with sugar or water sweetened with sucralose (Splenda). The scans showed that sugar activates the reward center of the brain while sucralose does not.

For this reason, artificially sweetened food and drinks don't fully satisfy cravings for natural sugar in the pleasure/reward center of brain. Ultimately, the artificially sweetened food leaves you craving more.

Sucralose is not the only bad guy. Another study found that Aspartame (Equal) is yet another source for increased cravings and a motivation to eat. Acesulfame K (Sunett, Sweet One), and Saccharin (Sweet'N Low, Necta Sweet) also have the same effect on the brain.

AminoSweet and NutraSweet are two of the newer names for Aspartame.

Finally, because artificial sweeteners are so much sweeter than natural sugar, it confuses up your taste buds. Over time you will require sweeter and sweeter foods and beverages to 'feel like' you are tasting something sweet.

Note: If your cravings persist, please consult with your doctor to determine if nutrient deficiencies and/or hormones could be the cause. Many people can develop nutrient deficiencies (even when they have a healthy diet). It's common to have hormonal fluctuations and/or imbalances at different stages of our lives. Look for a doctor that specializes in this area.

Testimonial

"When I met Diane, she was giving a presentation on sugar to a small networking group. She demonstrated how much sugar in a soda bottle by putting the same amount of sugar in an empty water bottle and then added a little water to show how the sugar hardens and sticks to the bottle. While I haven't had a soda in 20 years I was blown away and interested in learning more so I hired Diane for a 4 week program where for 1 hour per week, I was schooled on the basics of food. I learned more in those 4 hours than I did in all my years of health classes. I would say that you should hire Diane and get familiar with what you should be putting in your body."

-Jason Bass
Websites & Online Social Media
Owner of Jason Hunter Design, LLC

I have another special gift for you…

A complimentary copy of my

Sugar Jail Journal Sheet
so you can calculate the number of sugar grams you are consuming each day.

Email me at: diane@dianebmorris.com for your free copy!

Diane B. Morris

CHAPTER 6—STAND OUT

Making a great first impression is important to us all. Impressions or judgements are made quickly sometimes within seconds.

When your personal brand is present it exhibits your positive energy. Wearing colors and makeup that light you up—paying careful attention to your body language and deliberately portraying your confidence—will allow you to stand out in a crowd.

You determine what that first impression will be even before you speak.

Your body language and the way you dress, act and communicate make a huge difference even though you are not at a corporate interview.

Your prospects are visually interviewing you to decide whether they want to engage with you. A great deal of Know, Like and Trust is made within that first impression.

In addition you are interviewing them to see if you want to further a possible relationship with them.

Interview Statistics

Nonverbal communication during an interview:

- 67% failed to make eye contact
- 47% of interviewees had little knowledge of the company.

Do your homework!

Statistics of How First Impressions Are Determined

- 55% by the way you dress, act and walk through the door or enter a room
- 38% by the quality of your voice, grammar and of course the confidence you portray
- 7% by the words you choose

Color accounts for approximately 60% of the acceptance or rejection of what the other person sees.

Research estimates a lasting impression is made within the first 7-90 seconds.

When You Receive a Compliment

Always say thank you no matter how you feel about the statement. A non-positive response like 'oh this old thing?' negates a compliment. Practice saying thank you in the mirror or in the car so it becomes a natural response. When you receive a compliment such as, "I love your dress." graciously receive it with a "Thank you!" This quick response allows you to stand out in the crowd.

Color Analysis

Color analysis is based on your skin type, body type and your hair. When you choose an outfit from your closet or your outdoor clothing, it is important to know which colors compliment your physical traits, personality and style.

Most women do not realize the benefits of having their colors done. This process saves both time and money and has priceless value when it comes to choosing clothes they will actually wear.

Colors affect our mood. Our personal and professional goals are accomplished for long term success when we choose the right colors—whether it's for our wardrobe, shoes, accessories, hair or makeup.

Benefits of Color Analysis

- Look happier because you have pride in your personal and professional image

- Less fidgeting with your clothes. The clothes you choose will fit your body and you will look amazing

- Send a subliminal message that you're the person to speak to and listen to

- More self-assured because you look professional, talented and confident

- You can now focus on your business and the message you want your image to convey

- Depending on your height preferences you can look taller or shorter

- Easily camouflage body flaws

- Have the illusion of a defined waistline
- Instinctively choose pieces that are completely YOU

Your wardrobe is a mirror reflection of **who you are:** your likes, interests, inspirations and dreams.

Your appearance is the very essence of your personal authentic self.

Clients and others will be attracted to you as your new image sends the right and engaging message.

REMEMBER

You never have a second chance to make a great first impression!

CHAPTER 7—WARDROBE

General research states that women describe their wardrobe as...

- 20% of the clothes don't fit
- 50% of the clothes are way too ugly
- 10% of the clothes are worn too many times
- 20% of the clothes are pajamas

Necklines and Necks

Your neckline is likely to make all the difference between a look that flatters your figure, your height and your face shape. The neckline complements one's body shape and style. The right neckline can make you appear taller, slimmer and more stylish. When thinking about your neck or the neckline of your outfit, factor in your bust size. Think about how you want to be perceived and choose necklines that complement your existing wardrobe. Certain necklace styles look better with different necklines. Suits look fantastic with V-neck button-down shirts, skirts complement a draped or plunging neckline and square neck or boat neck look great with jeans. When you're looking for your great staple dress or top, pay attention to what kind of neckline will be most flattering for your body.

For plus size women, whether you're having fun with your friends or at work, there are many different flattering necklines that can change the way your bust, neck and face areas look. The cut of the neck opening, including the collar or trim can make or break the way you look, even if the rest of the top or dress is great.

Focusing on one's neckline is one of the simplest ways to highlight your assets. For example, if you are considered a plus size, some women who have a wide neck wouldn't want to wear something that will make the neck look thicker, nor would a woman with a small face want to create a disproportioned look from top to bottom.

A round face looks rounder in a rounded scoop neck. A square jaw stands out by wearing a square neckline. A long thin face, looks longer in a narrow V-neck. **A contrasting neck line balances your face.**

Short Neck

If your neck is short, an open collar, V-neck or scoop neck works best. Avoid high or stand up collars, turtlenecks or cowl necks. A crew or mock turtle neck is a better option. Short hair is best because it creates the illusion of distance between your head and shoulders. Choose soft scarves and a smaller size scarf to avoid having bulk around the neck.

Wide Neck

To minimize, keep a jewel or crew neckline close to the base of your neck on both sides.

Long Neck

If your neck is too long, a short hair cut will emphasize its length. It is best to add length, especially in the back and avoid deep-V-necklines. Options include scarves, a mandarin collar and a choker type necklace.

ACCESSORIES

Accessories make a personal statement to reflect your style. Accessories include shoes, handbags, jewelry, necklaces, scarves, hats and belts. Accessories should add to and not take away from your overall style. **Pick no more than 3 accessories to wear when going to an interview.**

Scarves

Scarves are an essential part of any wardrobe. They bring the right color to your face while you are phasing the wrong colors out of your wardrobe. Scarves come in a variety of colors, sizes, fabrics and shapes designed for different purposes. Scarves are fun. Wear them over your outfit or any outerwear.

Scarves can range in price-from a thrift store rack or a department store sale to a high end boutique. Search online to find the many ways to tie your scarf and remember to take your body shape, style and purpose into consideration.

Jewelry

Generally, there are 3 types of jewelry: gold, silver and gem stones.

- Gold is usually worn with the Warm colors such as reds, oranges, yellows.

- Silver is usually worn with the Cooler colors. Brown tends to be work best with silver. Greens, black, grays, whites, navy blue can go either way.

- Gem stones create a more formal look and are usually worn with sheer or shiny fabrics as well as velvet.

You can wear the same outfit and go from a casual to dressy to formal look just by focusing on your jewelry.

- Casual is better matched with the shiny group which includes gold or silver earrings, informal pins, casual necklaces or simple bracelets.

- Dressy is better matched with the brushed look in the metal or pearls. This includes brushed metal or pearl earrings, brushed metal pin, dressy bracelet or ring.

- Formal is better matched with earrings, pearls or gem stones from your color palette. Bracelets and rings with gem stones add sparkle to your outfits.

Choose your earrings first, chains and necklaces second, bracelets next, then the ring, and a pin last.

Handbags

It is essential you choose the one that is right for you. You probably wear this accessory more than any other accessory and you may be carrying your handbag through more than one season. The right handbag should flatter your figure, complete your personality and your perfect outfit.

The wrong shape and weight could cause shoulder, back, hips and foot trouble. Avoid bulky shoulder bags that sit around the middle part of your torso because this adds bulk and calls attention to that particular part of the body.

Handbags and Body Shape

- If you have small hips, choose a bag which hangs at the level of your hips because this will give you a curvier, more feminine look
- If you have large hips, choose a bag which hangs at your waist line to avoid accentuating your hips

Handbags that sit at the waist level will flatter most shapes. It's always good to have a bag of this type in your wardrobe.

- If you are tall and slim choose a handbag which is rounded or a slouch shoulder bag/satchel
- If you are short and curvy a handbag with strong angles will look great on you

Another important aspect in choosing the right handbag is to think about the purpose for the bag and what compartments/pockets you will need.

Body Shape

Most women focus on the problem areas of their body such as tummy, hips, waist line, bust, double chin and thighs. It is more important to see one's body as a whole picture.

Knowing your body shape will help you identify the patterns and type of clothing that will flatter you.

Recognizing Your Own Body Shape

Look at your body in the mirror when you are naked because even underwear can disguise your body shape.

Focus on the shape of your torso—shoulders to hips.

How do your shoulders compare to your waistline and your hips?

Is your weight equally distributed?

Here are the typical body shapes to notice. Inverted Triangle, Hourglass, Apple, Pear and Rectangle.

Inverted triangle

- Shoulders wider than hip line
- Sporty, model, and athletic type
- Hips look straight
- Little or no waist definition

Hourglass

- Hips and shoulders same width
- Waistline smaller

Apple

- Shoulders and hips line up and are about the same width
- Waistline same size or wider than shoulders and hips

Pear

- Waistline smaller than hips
- Gains weight evenly
- Hips wider than shoulders and waistline

Rectangle

- Lean look
- Little waist definition
- Straight balanced hips and shoulders

CHAPTER 8—COLOR

Color is Energy

Our appearance is actually an energy force utilizing color.

When you walk into the room, the colors you are wearing, your smile and your energy are the first things people notice.

Have you ever seen an individual who you don't know walk in the room and you could actually feel their exciting persona? They have a WOW factor going on.

Color is Actually Light

Color therapy or light therapy, is also known as Chromotherapy. Color therapy is an astonishing alternative of medicines for health maintenance whether it is a physical or mental reaction to light.

Color (light) enters through the eyes, but it also enters into our body through the skin—positively affecting different parts of our body.

It is said that a therapist trained in Chromotherapy, can use light in the form of color to balance 'energy' wherever a person's body is lacking, whether on the physical, emotional, spiritual or mental level.

This therapy is a part of ancient cultures of India, China and Egypt. It is based on a spectrum of light, each color having its special effects, energy and wavelengths.

Colors also have an important impact on a person's personality.

Chakra is a Sanskrit word which means 'wheel'.

The human body is said to include hundreds of concentrated and focused energy centers.

There are seven major chakras or energy centers. Each chakra is similar to a wheel that is spinning. Our chakras are where we receive, transmit and process energy. This is very similar to the nervous system which receives and transmits information, but the chakras receive, transmit and process energy within our etheric body.

Going from the tail bone to the top of the head, the colors of our chakras are red, orange, yellow, green, blue, indigo and violet. These are actually the colors in a rainbow.

As you can see these colors carry a lot of weight when we want to improve our mood, creativity, vitality, productivity, de-stress and send out positive energy.

CHAPTER 9—COLOR ANALYSIS

There are so many benefits to having your colors done. This is called Color Analysis.

Color analysis is based on your skin tone, body type and hair.

Most women do not realize how much money they can save by having their colors done. This analysis also saves time, closet space and improves your mood. Personal and professional goals are easily accomplished when we feel confident, healthy and powerful.

The Personal Power of Color

Below is a list of positive changes I attain when wearing the right colors for me.

- Under eye circles look less pronounced
- Facial lines are diminished
- Skin has a healthy and more radiant glow
- Eyes look sparkling and clear
- Hair looks shinier and healthier
- Appearance looks rested, instead of tired and/or stressed
- Nose appears smaller
- Body looks thinner and younger

Wardrobe Building & Color

Wardrobe building helps you to successfully stand out in the crowd and creates your personal brand. Knowing which colors light up your face while brightening your eyes and teeth is done best through color analysis.

In order to determine your own color palette you will need to understand how to figure out if you are what is called a Cool tone or a Warm tone.

Everyone has a dominant color in their skin that is either Cool or Warm. **There are 3 ways to determine whether you look best in the Cool colors (blue tones) or Warm colors (golden tones).**

The 1st way is to look at your skin color.

If your skin is dominantly any of these colors you are a Cool tone.

- Pink
- White
- Neutral Beige
- Olive
- Blue-Black

If your skin is dominantly any of these colors you are a Warm tone.

- Ivory
- Peachy
- Reddish
- Golden-Beige
- Golden-Black
- Golden-Bronze

The 2nd way is to look at your eye color.

If your iris is dominantly any of these colors you are a Cool tone.

- Cool dark brown

- Gray-blue
- Gray-green
- Blue
- Hazels (brown, green spec mixes with some gray effects)
- Gray
- Soft brown
- Taupe

If your iris is dominantly any of these colors you are a Warm tone.

- Golden-brown
- Rich dark-brown
- Warm hazels— combinations of specs of gold, moss greens, browns, yellows, greens, aqua, clear blue, and light golden-brown.

The 3rd way is to look at your veins.

Look at the veins in your wrist and arms in sunlight or lamp light.

- If your veins are of a bluish color then you are a Cool tone.
- If your veins are of a greenish color then you are a Warm tone.

Once you've determined if you are of the Cool or Warm tones you can determine your complimentary colors for your wardrobe.

Image consultants usually give their clients a matching color palette to accomplish this goal.

My clients and I have so much fun choosing their best colors!

CHAPTER 10—HAIR, SKIN & MAKEUP

Hair Color & Skin Tone

Let's talk about natural hair color and how it corresponds to your skin tone.

Cool Hair Color

- Ash brown
- Blue-black
- Medium to dark brown
- Gray
- Salt & pepper
- Platinum
- Ash-blonde
- Cool dark brown

Warm Hair Color

- Red
- Auburn
- Chestnut
- Copper
- Golden-brown
- Golden-blonde
- Yellow-blonde
- Golden-gray
- Strawberry-blonde

Hair Color & Haircut

The wrong hair color and or haircut will make you look…

- Older
- Unhealthy
- Tired

The right hair color and haircut will make you look…

- Younger
- Slimmer

Your Face Shape & Hair Style

Face shapes can change due to age and weight. Women who have round faces and lose 25+ pounds can end up with an entirely different face shape.

We all have one of 6 face shapes: Round, Square, Long (Oblong), Heart, Diamond or Oval.

Women tend to be hard on themselves. It can be dangerous to our self-confidence to find and consciously dwell on what we think is a flaw but it is truly something not one person notices when they look at us. While many women obsess with their face shape, there are other factors to consider before getting a new hairstyle.

It is important to consider your hair texture, lifestyle, personality, body shape and what you want in other words, your preferences.

Face Shapes & Hair Lengths

You can choose a haircut that will flatter your face shape.

Long (Oblong) Shape—Your face is obviously longer than it is wide and includes a large forehead

Heart Shape—You have a wide face and a pointy chin

Round Shape—You might have a short neck or a double chin

Square Shape—Your jaw is angular, as long as it is wide

Oval Shape—Your face is more egg shaped

Oval Shaped faces look good with any haircut, but these faces can appear long. The best hair cut will be accomplished when your hair stylist gives your face the oval shape illusion.

If you have a square face you may want to down play your strong, angular jaw. Texture, in the form of curls or choppy ends, does this brilliantly.

Heart shaped faces tend to come with pointy chins. Draw attention to your eyes and cheekbones instead.

Shoulder-length hair styles are universally the most flattering on nearly everyone.

Long hair—Generally means below the shoulders. Women who generally shouldn't go long are super-short people and women with long, narrow faces.

Women who look fabulous in long cuts have oval or square faces. That said, anyone with hair below their breasts is taking a risk of looking outdated.

Short hair—Comes in a variety of lengths. In order to figure out which length works for you, consider your best and worst assets and your height. Super short hair on very tall women can look masculine or it can look very powerful.

Short hair on women with round faces can make the round face appear fuller. Typically you'll want to grow your hair longer than your chin if you have a round face.

If you have a pointy chin, avoid hair that falls right at the chin. If you have great eyes, consider short hair with side-swept bangs that hit right at the eye.

Remember, a good hair cut masks your downfalls and promotes your best features.

One-length hair is great for super-fine hair, but doesn't work on everyone. Long layers are the key to the perfect haircut because they add body to flat hair, texture to thick hair and control to curly hair.

Layers should be cut in the front to frame the face. If you have short hair don't let your stylist cut layers above the eye. If you have long hair, never allow layers above your earlobe or you risk a dated look.

Skin Care & Makeup

Before applying makeup in the morning, wash your face so you'll be able to start with a fresh canvas and reduce skin blemishes.

Use a cleanser or simply splash lukewarm water on your

face a few times to wash away any 'leftovers' on your skin. Pat it dry gently with a soft towel.

Avoid washing your face with hot water. This will dry it out and leave it prone to irritation and infection.

Lukewarm water is best when you're washing your face.

Don't scrub your face dry. This causes fragile facial skin to lose its elastin over time.

It's not necessary to exfoliate every day, but doing so every few days is essential to keeping your skin looking fresh. Putting makeup on over dry, flaky skin defeats the purpose! Exfoliate your skin using either a small facial brush, an exfoliating scrub or another exfoliating tool designed for use on the face. Focus on areas that tend to get dry and flaky.

Using a face mask from time to time is another good way to keep your facial skin in good shape. Choose a clay mask, which will cleanse your pores and help pull off dry skin when you wash it away.

The last step before applying makeup is putting on some moisturizing lotion. This will help your makeup go on more easily and create a better final look. Choose a good face moisturizer that works with your skin type. Massage it gently all over your face. Don't forget your eyelids, lips and nose.

Let the moisturizer absorb into your skin for a few minutes before you move on to applying your makeup. Putting makeup on while your face is still wet or sticky will result in a mess!

The Casual Everyday Look

Ready to feel fresh and confident as you go about your day?

Everyday makeup should cover blemishes, define your bone structure and highlight your pretty eyes without making you look overdone.

If you want a natural, but polished appearance: Apply foundation and powder, light eye makeup and a neutral lipstick.

Foundation must match the tone of your skin in order to look natural where it ends and your neck begins. Choose a foundation that works with your skin type and matches your coloring. Liquid foundation is a good choice for many types of skin. You can also use tinted moisturizers. If your skin is on the oily side, you might want to consider compact or powder foundation.

Test your foundation to make sure it matches your face by dabbing a little on your jaw bone. Never apply it on the back of your hand as the skin color there is different from your face.

Apply the foundation evenly over your face using a foundation brush, pad or your finger. Make sure it doesn't cake or clump anywhere.

Blend the foundation around the edges of your face and where it meets the bottom of your chin.

Note: Avoid putting extra layers of foundation over blemishes. It will only make them stand out more.

Only use concealer to cover your blemishes. Foundation first, then concealer.

Concealers can be used if you have dark under-eye circles. If so, use a concealer that is one shade lighter than your foundation. Apply a light amount of concealer using either a concealer brush or your ring finger. Dab it under your eyes and gently blend it in. This will make your eyes look bright instead of sleepy and give you a healthier look.

If you're trying to pare down your makeup routine, you can skip the concealer. It all depends on which features you want to play down and which you want to highlight.

Use a little extra concealer on blemishes if necessary—making sure to use a color that matches your skin tone.

Bronzer should be applied with a small fluffy brush or an angled powder/contouring brush. Apply it around the hairline, under the cheekbones, around the jawline and under the chin. Bronzer can give you a healthy glow. If you have dark skin, just stick to a highlighter.

Contour is the perfect way to make your face appear structured and slim—provided you do it right! Use a powder or foundation two shades darker than your skin-tone. Apply it down the sides of your nose, under the cheekbones, around the hairline, jawline and chin using an angled powder brush or your fingers if using a cream product.

Blush comes after applying bronzer & contour using a blush brush. Apply blush to the apples of your cheeks and blend upwards.

Note: Contrary to popular belief blush should not be applied while smiling, it will actually drag your features down.

Eyeliner is the cosmetic which is used to define the eyes. It provides a dramatic look. It is a perfect instrument to reshape the eye. Eyeliner is found in liquid, powder based pencil and wax based pencil.

Mascara is the cosmetic which is applied on the eyelashes to make them thicker and darker. It helps to enhance the eyes. Different types of mascara can be found in the market. Water proof mascara can help to retain the curl and prevent smudging.

There are many resources for your skin care and makeup. Finding a company and consultant who will be there to answer questions and who knows about your skin care needs and what looks great on your face is essential to keeping your face looking healthy.

I have a resource in case you are looking for a reliable, dependable and always reachable skin care consultant.

Diane B. Morris

CHAPTER 11—STYLE

Style is about design, manner, variation and interpretation. When choosing your wardrobe you can decide what style you love and feel good about no matter what body type you have. You might identify with one or a combination of these main styles.

Classic

- Neutral palette for makeup
- Defined cheekbones
- Defined brows
- Mascara
- ***The Gwenyth Paltrow Style***

Dramatic

- Self-confident
- Defined makeup
- Face, artist's palette
- Dramatic hairstyle, but does not work as a style you wear everyday
- Black heels
- ***The Beyonce, Oprah, Whitney Houston & Kardashian Style***

Elegant

- Fills the room with their presence
- Polished
- Neutral make up
- Lip and eye make-up are soft
- ***The Katy Holmes & Jennifer Anniston Style***

Natural

- Wholesome look
- Minimal makeup
- Minimal lipstick, mascara
- Comfortable clothing

- Simple hairstyles
- Hair loosely laying on shoulders
- **The Cameron Diaz & Reece Witherspoon Style**

Romantic

- Frilly, feminine clothing
- Soft makeup
- Pink, lavender colors
- **The Jennifer Love Hewitt Style**

Sporty

- Chic style
- Looks fabulous, not much time or thought put into their wardrobe
- Grey trousers, loafers, turtle neck, jacket
- Short, simple style hair-cut
- **The Ellen DeGeneres Style**

Personality + Wardrobe = Style

Your personality traits define how socially appealing you are to others. It's the way you portray yourself in social situations.

There are 5 main ways we appear to others, these are called Personality Factors.
1. Open
2. Conscientious
3. Extrovert, Introvert or Ambivert
4. Agreeable
5. Neurotic or Anxious

It is possible to change your personality factor and that is part of the work I do with my clients.

Your style becomes your personal brand. It is a combination of your personality as well as your wardrobe and how well put together you appear.

Your wardrobe reveals how attractive you will be to your target market. It is important that your personal life be aligned with your personal brand because you and your business are one.

"Your time is limited, so don't waste it living someone else's life. Don't be trapped by dogma—which is living with the results of other people's thinking. Don't let the noise of others opinions drown out your own inner voice. And most important, have the courage to follow your heart and intuition."

-Steve Jobs

Case Study & Testimonial

When Mary came to me she was uncomfortable in social situations, especially when standing up to introduce herself at networking meetings. She would experience anxiety when walking into a room of strangers.

"Diane Morris is passionate about helping others develop their own personal brand. I was a client of Diane through her 7 week 'BrandtasticYou' coaching program. During my time with Diane, I learned simple ways to improve my self-confidence as well as how to develop my Why for what I do and reach my goals—both personal and professional. Diane really helped to set my course as I launched my business and started the networking process. I highly recommend Diane and her 'BrandtasticYou' coaching program."

-Mary Buzzeo
AIPB Certified Bookkeeper
Owner of Journals and Ledgers, LLC

CHAPTER 12—PERSONAL BRANDING

My Story

From a very young age, I felt I didn't fit in. I became a 'people pleaser'. This continued throughout my adult life. I eventually experienced a serious emotional and health crisis.

The following year I was involved in a near death car accident. I realized then, that life is too short and I needed to initiate a serious 'life makeover'. I left the corporate world and combined my nutrition expertise, years of self-development and my love for fashion to create **'BrandtasticYou'**. Through this personal branding coaching program, women regain their confidence, look fantastic and restore their authentic best self.

My holistic business philosophy of personal branding places more emphasis on understanding yourself and the needs of others. When you meet the needs of others, while staying true to your values and continuously improving yourself, you will see tremendous everlasting growth in your life and career.

I love this quote from Dr. Suess: "Today you are you! That is truer than true. There is no one alive who is 'youer' than you!.." 18 words that describe personal branding to a 'T'!!

'BrandtasticYou'

My customized personal branding program, 'Brandtastic You', uncovers your special gifts, talents and expertise in a way that is comfortable and authentic to you. This unique coaching program and system will transform your personal and professional life.

This amazing system includes formulas and assessments to make sure your authentic self is rediscovered. The information attained allows me to empower you to build your confidence through wardrobe, color and style.

'Brandtastic You' is a 3 Pillar personal branding program that includes Your Strong Confident Self, Your Optimal Nutritional Self and Your Brilliant Colorful Self.

My Mission

To help women uncover their natural talents that match their personality and physical traits so they can be confident, content and comfortable as they enter new crossroads in their personal and/or professional life.

Build Your Confidence Through Wardrobe, Color & Style

Looking to uncover your next step?

Schedule a

Complimentary

'Brand New You' Strategy Session

with me at: dianebmorris@dianebmorris.com

To Your Best Health,

Diane

www.brandtasticyou.com

Diane B. Morris

ABOUT THE AUTHOR

Diane Morris is an Image Consultant and Registered Licensed Dietitian. She received her B.S. in Foods and Nutrition at the University of Utah and completed her dietetic internship at the University of Alabama, Birmingham. Diane is also a Neuro Linguistics Practitioner and a Dr. William Sear's Health Coach. She is certified in Adult Weight Management and Children's Self Esteem.

Diane spent over 27 years in the corporate health care arena and due to her unexpected life experiences, she left corporate to follow her dream and start her own business. She combined her nutrition expertise, years of self-development, and her love for fashion to create **'BrandtasticYou'**. Through this personal branding coaching program, women regain their confidence, look fantastic, and restore their authentic best self.

Diane B. Morris

Manufactured by Amazon.ca
Acheson, AB

14834694R00057